Conjugal

by

Alicia Vandevorst

Poetic Matrix Press
www.poeticmatrix.com

Acknowledgments

To phonemes,
To the teachers who prefer to remain nameless,
To the gardens in Ganeshpuri,
To my dad,
To my mom,
To Kitty,
To these poets: Kim for help with recitation,
her crosscheck of my Ophelia, and our talks,
To Iven for sharing the word-drink that
pours out of his rich, complex barrel and his feedback,
early and late, on this set of poems,
To Rachel for water-time, the muse drawing,
NanoWrimo, and various kinds of balm,
To Maxima for our low-light Sunday afternoons and
your help with three of the poems in here,
To Gene for reading this book at least four times,
for your questions, your musings,
our clarifying conversations, and for sharing
so many themes; you encouraged me to
take the time I needed with those poems that
confounded me, also, for the book on Yeats's forms,
To Archna for her bone and flower gifts,
To Ariana and her overgrown pool and casita,
the peace there,
To Mariana for our walks and moonlight readings,
To Crystal, Rachel, Shanta, and Tera, and your children:
each of you restores my faith, one way or another,
To my children, Iris and Serena, Serena and Iris,
who are my intimate wonders; I intend this book
to be one way to share my heart with you
when I cannot be there,
To Toon for our life together, including
all the warm beverages and countless
hours you spent reading and commenting on my drafts,
To all those whose risks uphold tenderheartedness,
And to any overlooked,
May the right blessings
reach you.

Contents

Conjugal

Conjugal

Yet I have been to Eden daily
and when I'm there I rip its roughage off,

eat hearts of lettuce fistful after fistful…

Guest

I would welcome you. I would bathe your feet. You would
sit on a cushion and show your nubile, smooth toes, or if it is
you, your callouses from boots, or your ingrown nails. I will
bathe them, place them, wet in the lamplight, on a plush towel,
or scrap of burlap, and hold them for a moment only, an instant,
then I will lower them to the floor slowly one by one and look
up into your eyes, green, brown, blue.

I will offer my voice to you, once we are seated. I will sing to you
like this: as I pour your tea, my hand will tremble. That is a song.
As I smile and answer how, how, and then why, more and more
songs will brush into you and how the dry part of you will crack
away, how the open places will feel lonely and good, and why
the day will touch you more than ever. We will find time for
questions. We will watch our lives without despair. I will sing.

Here is a song:

O the sun and the old stump, they meet right there
and do not run, but burn. The heat of the sun sits.
The old stump sits and does not speak,
but the chipmunk does. Its leg is broken.
It peeps and struggles. The cat is there to swat it into the grass.
My heart is with the chipmunk. My heart is with the cat.
My heart is with the old stump. My heart is with the sun.
My hands are still.
My hands are still.

Alternate Eve

You rise from an adamantine ground of silence,
rich with unsaid shit, united sound;

you on the edge, in the middle, or changing tunes,
no one walks before you. No one bids

with glances; no one tills within your garden
since you stray everywhere,

alone and keen and sensitive to the coil
of spring in your own spine. So content

with every subject, you mate the present. You have
no reason to object. For in Eden,

strangeness is what the lover digests.

Your Puzzle

*—Asi is both a name for the ancient Mother Goddess Isis
and the personification of the first sword ever made,
according to Hindu epics.*

The future is no mother, maybe;

it does not arc itself to serve

singular prayers, so what
is the fulcrum of grace?

Think of John Jihadi's hands.
How many prayers circle them and seek

entrance to his nervous system?
And he beheads; the hand of god

(Asi, are you aware?) takes
the heads of other gods.

Dream: Some Intestines Ache with Diamonds

From the street, a woman's shouts enter my dream and change
every color and the language spoken. Her screams build a stairway
that curves so fully the end is out of sight. I walk up her long
escalation of green, which is down a dead clean bone with finely
carved banisters, and both arrive in semi-darkness where silhouettes
fall together like roughage in a stomach. I feel the eye
that is hers and mine, digested down to a common light. But as I wake,
the plain cotton on my skin, the roundness of my forearm like
sticky white bread stops the whole evacuation.

You, You, You, and You and You

If you'd let me, Donald, I'd place you, lounging alone, in
an aisle of cherry trees in spring, to watch their canopies tear
and fall to a sweet litter that will moulder and brown, to see
the pink, incandescent petals, so many billions, flutter and fly,
be prone beneath them, absorbed in brightness, and then lose them.
It is okay to lose. That shimmer, like any woman's ass, like the
Appalachian mountains, the sleepy Catskills, will go flat and plain.

Polish

When young, the son of a former president rode his
mare in the Cinco de Mayo parade. Her golden and
graceful neck arched like a laurel tree, and the singing,
the shaking banners, nothing ever caused a misstep.
He thought her an excellent partner for the tricks he did
on her back. Till that day, when toward the end of the parade
a sudden firecracker spooked her and she slipped
on the stones. He leapt clear, but she broke, screaming.
Everyone stood about gawking, unwilling to act. So
he drew his gun and shot her between the eyes.

I have valued my partner's decisiveness. Today, we tour his
new clinic, planning each room. Outside, in bright-eyed talk, he leaps
up onto a low wall. So I leap, too, but miss and slip hard, can barely
stand. He narrows his eyes then strides home, leaves me bleeding.

When I find him upstairs, he is cleaning his gun.

Orange

I cannot find the answer and circle
like a songbird who misses the light
of a faint, perfect guide; that remains so
perfect, out of sight in the orange,
stagnant maze. And they die
of exhaustion, the songbirds.
Our need for illuminated night
creates a vortex of star-birds
with throats ample and free, delivered
to music but they fall, their light bones
are small matted wastes in the city.

Tired Sonnet

Tired as the apple, waterless,
whose bark is sloughed by the wind yet bears,
atop two branches, fruits like yes,
said sweetly, desperately, to life's own flare,

I go. Tired with tasks to do, I go,
as fingers chafe like fraying rope and burn.
As nothing steadies, it is hard to bow,
to look past my groundless hopes and learn.

Look through the layers of stored material—
the bark, the gathered options, are they barren?
Or will there be a welcome, an ethereal
redemption? Or am I wholly mistaken?

What if all I thought to give is false?

Widow Briar Edits Her World

Once there was a woman with a yard full of roses.
As she aged, she could not tend so many.
The ones she could not tend, she let go wild
in weeds and scraggly grasses, and under their own weight
they drooped and went to hips quickly.
But she did not seem to see that part of her yard.
She never looked up at me across the abandoned side.
She tended and pruned a smaller and smaller space,
and, there, she gave herself completely.
Not a weed, not a dead bloom lingered there.
And then it was only a row of roses
along the path to her door.
Then it was one bush,
beside the low porch,
as if the single plant
was an entire garden.

Blankies

There were four, and each gave a particular comfort. The yellow of my favorite one resembled cooked spaghetti squash. Its cotton had shredded at the edges, but its power formed a second, golden skin, and it accumulated strength from places: Baskin Robbins, the Book Mobile, Night Hall, the rose garden in Elizabeth Park, and that farthest playground behind the rose garden, which was in the young forest and had an overcast quality to the metal in the braces for those swings, like loneliness and quietude at once. In the fabric, I felt the marble of official entryways and the deep bins of spicy powders, dried fruits, and beans in the tiny food co-op, the densely packed shelves there, the Panda licorice's brown-when-bitten edges, the barns we passed on the way to Simsbury, old Talcott Mountain.

The blankie absorbed the mountain itself, too, with its slow-winding, wide trail through yellowed maples with hand-sized leaves thickly shaking overhead, the sumac's jaunty blood-red spikes, dead red, and later the black of pond-water, the moisture of worms, the tangle of earthworms in dad's bait can, the hooks with black accumulations of fish mouth and worm skin, the poorly lit cellar of salvaged furniture, chairs with three legs, frames, mirrors, lamps, all in some sort of shambles, all with potential for hybrid form; all of this sunk into the yellow blankie.

It was my keeper of largeness and power, but I lost it. I left that yellow one in Boston, somewhere in the Museum of Natural History, and some time after that bus trip my mom tried to get rid of all of the blankies. But I hunted them, found them in the trash, insisted she allow them. She made me choose one. The other two, a blue and a pink one, went out in the trash the next morning.

I had one, then, the white one with the grape stain in its corner and the good curl along its edge, good for getting under my nails and sustaining my nervous habits. I did not think of how disgusting I must have been to grown ups; I felt kind with that blankie in hand. The white one had blue and pink stripes an inch from the edge, but I don't remember it new; it was faded and only roughly rectangular by the time I studied it apart from the others. It was soft, threadbare, and closer to gray than white by then.

It was gentleness and friendship. It could sustain my love songs to the backyard meadow and endure; it once rode the back bumper of Dad's blue Volkswagen bus on his long commute from Hartford to New Haven for three days in a row. Then we found it tucked there, unharmed. It was hard to let my mom wash it ever. I loved the harbor of smells that blankie became. It was part of the connection—the saliva, tears—but she insisted finally. I understood her need in the way I understood obedience. But it ruined things for me, until I could write poems.

My Cat, There

I placed within her frame precisions
that I refused to bring to language,
the rover in me, the sleeper, the silence,
and the careful tongue. She did all
as I attended, as if my life
was an observance, a following.
I could watch the world batted
like mice, while safe as warm glass.
She curled away the tender part
of me, or strutted it through meadows,
aloof and agile in trees, or spooked.
Night was hers—the bulletin of blue
that said nothing to me but *there, there.*
She read the scents and left me docile.
She hunted through the shadows in
the knowing mud. I only saw
her groom her feet patiently,
thoroughly, in a patch of sunlight.

Mistake

Between the birches
and apartments,
a yellow swallowtail
and a yellow leaf

circle closer, and flutter their
indistinguishable
lobes giddily
in a long spiral,
lowering,
until they
brush.

Then dazedly the
butterfly bobs, propels itself up,
over, making its way,

as the yellow leaf
spins down
to join
the litter.

Before the Trip to Orange

~ My last dinner with Dad

You lean on padded elbows and purse your lips and blow
slowly through, and draw the air, haul the air,
so slowly, barely back. You laugh, and as we bless the food
you cry, not for yourself, for tiny, soft peas,
for the few easy breaths, for our hands in yours.

Later I sit and place my head on your knees.
My hair is shoulder length, and your hands go to my nape,
though you barely have the strength to stroke my skin,
your rough fingers want this, the father's touch,
to soothe her off to sleep—

Your knees so bony they burn my skull, and those cracked
fingers only scratch, but I am silent, let you caress
until you hardly have any breath
and need to let go.

In Orange

She said the eye of the needle
is the passage to the white crown
of sanctity. How slender a thing
must be to meet that moon.

Almost a song, as thin as that,
and nobody, no body can slip
the noose and fly, until the drip,
the feed of nectar has unleashed

its bolt from cell to cell and changed
the waiting one into a silver cord
and the light in the room unnerves
the sense of time and you say

Goodbye within the golden wake
of the unpacked soul, to the
rough sack of his face, and grip
his fallen hand,

and sing after that open door
O love o love o love
and whether praise or pain what else
can be named when you almost follow?

The Seal

I'd dispersed,
with little left in the feet,

life defrayed to the gardens,
into the morning litter of immaculate champa flowers,

to jasmines, cannonball, and pipal trees.
The dark spears of the rudraksha leaves are breathing.

The wiry teaks, dusty up the red mountainside,
wait for the rains.

The river in the middle carries away ashes and cows;

and then between the mango trees his hand rests in mine
but faintly, as water in a cloud, almost condensed.

I happen to be there when the groundskeeper comes,
so gently, quickly with the broken hive to the table.

A black carcass of wax.

He breaks a piece and lays it, dripping, in my hand.
The honey condenses the garden,

unites it on my tongue,
my life.

Our Mark

It's abloom, hell.

The perennial terrorism
displays cadaver-petals
with stamens of radioactive rubble
that dust its exposed pistils,
the orphaned, red-palmed children.

To the Spine in Winter

First it seemed unknown, an omnicolor, almost gray,
as vibrantly summing as the gloam that swallows the colorful rays.
We hunted through years; we combed our lives for what might catch
onto our hands, in the bone-dry grass we searched for a living patch;
but autumn tripped its bomb, and bodies flew to bits
that we piled up to steam, like moans, and we carved our lists of soldier breasts
onto a polished stone where the weather bangs its circling water;
all dead, all earth, the geomantic die we cast has rolled:
we missed the bones of what is larger than surety and gain,
and minded the maps of our own minds, the printed organs, the forced
mutations that outcast the omens of starlings;

so, dead bone, what amen shudders even now?

In winter, as the koan night delivers the light in darkness,

it is the crone who I uncover, the forgotten, she who

is dromedary; with her tankish cup concealed in drab, taut skin,

she endures. For the unheard drone may sweeten her walk and her

eyes though dark turn merry as proms, with odd quickness larger

than being subject to thrones or certainty, larger than

vertebrae like words; as a poem, she can

build a spine of foam as light and wild as bees, as sunrise

whose solemn rings are bedded in the loam, a spine so wise

it supports a hidden nomenclature derived from seeing

waves of intent rolling through entire scenes, not things.

First Order

I was once a blue shade who slipped through meadows,
only a hum like the one the heart makes as it sees
the edges erase in the dusk, though the grasses shift and brush
but now as one music; now the hand sets down the glass
and relaxes, and the moon will slowly rise in a time not kept
except by breathing, aimless breaths that cause no wishes.
I will not be banished from the scene by documents.

Where is the Queen of the Slaughter sitting these days?
Has she signed her scrawl again, is she sighing, as war
again descends from her mind into the lined world?
I am at her ear, saying, "Sovereign, sovereign,
love your children, love the edgeless meadow
of children, sovereign, sovereign," almost a hiss now,
"Sense…"

But she, the pitiless, wonder-less woman
who trusts only dividends to be secure, only
divisions, leans wanly sideways in her tight tower
and draws its tight circumference everywhere she looks, deciding,
deciding to stamp her domain's dimensions as the right.
You live within my circle. You live within my circle.
Here is my law, a ring of fire, a ring of fire!

Yet she hears me wordlessly—we are that intimate—
as she sees the thunderhead beyond her window, sees
her body in a lightning bolt, how its forked edges
stand out, yet it belongs to the cloud-field, and further,
the air, the billowing sphere in orbit, the continuous
dawn, conversant elements, the ripples of values,
all existing due to others' existence, and rendering her fortress

barren.

Thunderclouds

—dharmameghadhyana, *a Sanskrit term
that means the 'thundercloud of grace'.*

1

I used to stand on the porch to watch
the dark close over the green of summer.
The wind would gust through the grasses, and rake
the static pall of our conflicts up,
with the humid, hot air, to seed the thunderhead.
I would stand stripped of thought and wait
for the angles of rain.

Sometimes, I would break from the rail,
into the clear water,
to be washed and blend with the heightened scents
of grasses, yarrow, mint.
I would run as fast as the rain,
and splash barefoot in the puddles
on the hot slate sidewalk and lift my face.

After, I would walk in the glimmer,
the fresh, silent air
before another thunderstorm forms.

2

Always the wide green meadow moonlit beside the road.
Always the imaginary bird hidden in the skirting trees,
that sings, far off, of indigo and the pearly swell of being.
Always I walk into the field, a child who dreams a man
who wades through the knee-high grasses in black, and stands
within the winds of a sudden storm, caught but with arms outstretched.
I watch the lightning strike his head and feel its white wash,
the cool night grasses, barely wet, the dark circle
of trees, the birdsong as he falls gently to his knees.
Always I feel the extreme joy of the bolt and the damp,
sad darkness of his body. Always I wake and hold those two.

3

A tree that has been struck by lightning sometimes
bears a spiral cicatrice, sometimes splits,
and its shattered core weathers in rains.
Either way it is changed, (alive
or dead). So the ascent of insight shakes
the downward trend of selfishness and fear.
It seems to strike out of the heavens yet
it rips right up from under your feet.

4

Once I sat in the snow
facing a steep descent.

I do not recall the cold
only an old hand,

only the bolt that flowed
through my spine to open it.

I sat in the snow and knew
I am infinite.

O

Pale doe,
with dark eyes, wide,
fluidly serene,
eating songbird hatchlings.

Archipelago

1

I make dolls of pale green glass with their fine lips parted
and place behind those lips songs that you prompt by
breathing into their mouths. The glass bodies are built
like puzzle pieces that can be latched together to form
a sheltering wall where the light of day varies—bowls of
darker green, ribbings of brightness. These dolls are a solitary
joy, more permanent than vinyl, hard and transparent
and fragile. I shape these noses so that the nostrils open,
so that the eyes look widely with relaxed lids, so that the
beauty of light, that cycle, may animate their faces—
a thing I may accidentally shatter or bury beneath trees
or give to arms like a baby. But each is a fixed file of beauty,
a box for human song, as if the human heart were left as a trace,
possible to retrieve responsively.

2

On the saffron-slipcovered couch, we extend
our feet to each other, bare for rubbing. I wince as you press
a spot that would fall, if the foot were a spine, between
my navel and my heart. You say, pressing harder,
"There's a one-eyed orange monster here." And I think of
hot rice that wears the scent of another plant, saffron;
think of the oddness of silk, how we toss the spun cocoon into
boiling water, just like making tea, and the fibers release, unwind
easily for us; think of the potency of saffron orange, its vigorous
delicacy, I include the color of the couch in this instance of
release. Why is what I hold dear a monster?
Can my vigor be released delicately?

3

I broke the coconut beneath the willow tree. It cracked into
two white cups, open skyward, glistening. Like moons,
but like Jack's crown and the well water flying out, downhill,
what is deepest meets the dirt and gives what's needed,
teaches 'go ahead, be thrown open'.

4

circa 1957
Before that scene I swelled, a red sail at the tip of a triangle
of beaten brown dirt that sunk toward our white-washed out-
buildings with reports of guns still shattering and near, muddy
pools of blood my brothers my wards falling; I run red and wide,
and take a fallen Chinese gun, and fire on the soldiers left to loot
our temple; I fire on those beautiful humans who pierced hearts I
swore were protected; I scour the stupa, roaring like fire
taking fallen guns, until they all have bowed, limp hands; all those
bodies, I would otherwise kneel to and bathe in sweet water,
shriveling.

5

Raimundo Arruda Sobrinho was a homeless man who wrote poetry
on tiny pages that he kept within a folder bound by rubber bands.
His beard muffled his jaw, a tangled mane obscured his forehead,
and his skin developed lines and darkened: it is rare to see a face so
worn and yet not crushed to bitterness or absence. He wore black
garbage sacks for years, yet every page he dated and preserved with
a trust in inner fruitfulness. But what if a woman had never started to
converse, day by day, with him until he showed the poems to her, or
she had not been moved to act on his behalf, or his brother had not
found him, taken him home, or if no picture ever showed him shaven
and dapper, so that his eyes stood out, so that, years of
inconsequentiality having stripped them of petty rancor, his eyes
stood out: without the happy ending of modest renown would we
still agree that his life, his course had worth? How would he
answer that question?

6

She sits in the center of its porch, on the last of three steps, arms
on her knees. The house is under-thunderhead-blue and her wrap is
camellia pink. Her dress is white and plain. The porch, she swept,
and the room behind is sweet with herbal incenses and bare. For her,
death has come and gone. She serves tea and a fresh cake from her
oven. You sit on a pillow and the steam wavers on a current, wild.
An ocean has smoothed this place like driftwood.
The invisible ocean changes her hair, her creases, her words.

7

It is green broom that sits where the fire will be soon. Sparks like a hundred goldfish dart; crinkled flakes, they swirl into the damp cedar's gills. We all escape into a larger being as pendular as breathing. Even the stars are this sort of fish. The green broom whistles and coils, glowing orange. Black rakes of broom shrivel in the clear place in the fire. The fire sings.

Encomium, Not to the God Apart

O great fire, exact
in the order of mathematics,
the nature of agreements
like hydrogen and oxygen,
and how the jet stream flows
or who will wash the dishes,
and the patterning of neurons!

O you, tenderly careless
of losses, in us you react, act
every side, and win or loss,
the value is in accord with the vision
of the teller, and the confluence
of visions we profess, tweet,
and text and yet you wink when I shiver,
seeing lovely alignments, seeing
the equal way

your ground receives every footfall,
even the old light of stars.

You, the one dark owl
in the skittering moonlight,
sweet-faced and terrible,
take the beauties that I nest
in plans, on whose shoulders I want
to rest. Lingering,
the mind adopts foundations that you,

mercy of entirety,

render equal
to the minute tardigrade.
For no thing is more or less
for you; no thing deserves
worse care. And not one is
marked to last and be cherished,
kept as an undying, embodied vow.

The Queen Accepts Herself as Part and Whole

She had black arms as her white arms slept,
shadowy arms she pretended not to know.
Her white skin, her black skin, neither mattered
to these boneless arms—one pair greedy, the other sleeping.
The dark arms raised golden dreams of doors opening:
threshold after threshold crossed painlessly,
and hands shaking those vantablack fingers,
touching her rings, coy wrists in every direction, passing
her dark limbs further and further on, leaving her baby
like a piece of her own shadow, offering glasses of wine,
here, and a sip, here, and a laugh, here, and a nod, and a
new room, and in every exchange the whisper of stats.
She arrived at forty-five years old without a blemish,
pulled back from everything, Queen of Lies,
but her pale arms of moonlight are stirring.
Tenderly they unfold from the elbows like swan necks
and caress empty space, unconcerned with doorways.
They bob and sway and every room falls silent,
mouths open, no drinks are swallowed, through all the doors,
slowly the white arms wind through, lovers' arms
talking with each other the first time, gingerly brushing,
tracing marks that no one can see but the fingers know
will thrill, lazily wafting their bodiless gestures through;
and no one wants to live near them, rooms are darkening
ahead of them, paint peeling, places that cannot be sold,
shifting nervously, the whisperers recoil and are gone.
The dark arms shuddering, smoke or shadows behind flames,
the pale arms match them, cause them to dance outside,
moving outside the rooms to a field of darkness, where no one
can verify the worth of the gestures they make together.

Dream: From Her Three-forked Tongue

The night was something albumin
for the heat of dreams to shape.
She set aside her canny list and
drew her lyre between her legs.

Ripples, over the shoulders of the
sleeping men of Thebes, spread.
Where she could not tread in daylight
to seek our pain, she sprung at night;

she, the water's daughter, sang
from the wellspring, from the stain
of her dragon blood. From its guts
she strung her harp. Her tongue, suffuse
and tender, visited the earth.

Her secret heart would drive her.
Its empty-all would mix the white
to rainbow gray and light the black,
as she moves their dreams toward love.

Dream: Opening

Our bitter mother, she recoils,
curses the hooves of these dark horses
that race the narrow room
she painted a vast and fenceless desert.
Her invisible webs tangle and tax their legs
below their sleekness and free heads.

Now to spoil her curse
I pull an iron shoe from one
pounding, pointed hoof and take
a bite. It turns soft and sweet
I turn through the wall from the dull
room to a meadow and sky. I toss
the horseshoe in the air, and it breaks
into swallows which fly, a spray
of black, broken sickles.

Any Devotion

—*for the Sea Silk Mistress, Chiara Vigo,*
who maintains the ancient, devotional
practice of weaving byssus, for free.

Hey, wanderer, collect the saliva of clams.
Dive and crawl their calcified beds—like palms
the pale shells clasp and issue brown threads
into the dizzy-clear weight of sea-green water;
keep weighing your breath, till you rush
sleek and foamy through the salty heaves,
lick your lips as you break to air and speak
not at all. Exit and loaf and save
your voice for benefit.

Laugh, take the brown threads then sing
words that have been polished with love of the sea
to mirror the sea's own ways of change;
as they lift the dark to show the light within:
thread by thread, the sea silk is golden.

Altar

On this strand of shine, mid-air, I place my gifts

this morning I place tear-wet eyes, with the sun-blaze
that rose, and stroked the petals of a poem left in my mind,

and the sun became the corona of the bloom of poem I do not remember
perfectly, that is broken now after breaking into me:

an emptied bank of gold, a tumbled thing that is hidden, crippled,
curled across its sensitivity. Scathingly, the sun-poem that is not

about the sun, where there is no certainty of rebirth, where the self
absorbs itself, spends itself, and hides its greatness under the water

of tears, and years pass over the civilization of the heart that dwells
in its own musical depths, that are not struck by light, that are cold

and yet that Atlantis throbs, heart-like, in the imagination,
that dead-wood poem is so accurate a mirror

that the sun is in it. The cut bloom as the sun.
And I am defenseless, here, being cut and crying,

with storms of flame, leaping out into space, the phrases
of a poem of praise I could not frame, leaping back into the sun's face.

'Rta'

—The Vedic principle of natural order

No longer dainty or softly green, I flare
in this rite: my browned arms slope
like sunflower leaves that hang, useless,
as the flower-heads bulge and disclose the sun
that the plant has swallowed. My order
is silence, and all the head must do is burn—

with the art of being a human mother,
who bathes as if beside a black bear mother
who, no longer frightened of us, has brought
her cubs to play within cold lake water,
frolicking in shallows beside kayaks
and human toddlers; the art is of burning fear,

of letting bias depart by making only
seeds whose origin includes the sun,
the root system, the soil, a whole stem—
not spliced like a golem—and time
in silence: not the mere poetic allusion,
but the fasting state in which no noise
is allowed to shift the mind into
its current. Not the mere allusion to silence
as the restraint of the tongue, but such as after
days when the vibrations of the world
grow or subside, and I remain like the
hanging leaves both part of and yet
parting from the bustle, sweet and light
with dying.

Dragonfly

I see how still you are.

Your crumpled, complex body
clings in the messy wind

to the wagging twig,
as you draw the long course

of clear fluid from
wrinkled caves of abdomen

and slip it through that diaphanous
lattice of wings.

Nothing seems

to happen even
as the birds grow active

over the wicker-rough lake,
even as I lean closer

you adhere to your inward needs,
one-pointedly.

I watch how nothing seems to happen
yet it keeps your full attention,

how not even fear can force a move.

Conversion of Things into Songs
to Their Own Beings

Into this abdomen like a raised bed,
rich in soil: what would I sing as seeds
to sink in that silence? Outside: the abandon
of a pool-gone-green and the meaningless
lisps of bamboo in a hot, slow wind.
To translate them into a fertile song
to what presents this time and vision
seems irreverent yet needed like
digestion.

So pool, whose waters barely cross
the bottom step, and frog, whose sallow legs
I saw thrust backward as you went
below the greenly prosperous algae
which bloom beneath the reflected blue and spears
of bamboo leaves, and you weathered aqua,
you, dryness, and grosbeak, and unknown lark
whose winsome whistle pierces, but not like bowing,
once I have a song for you, I'll sing it,
tend it.

Dream: The Cave

As a tended fire lights
the vaulted cave with orange,
an austere, naked dancer
bends her gaze to her middle,
folds into a crescent,
and almost like the discus-thrower,
lifts her empty left hand
toward the dark. She does not know
the object of her love; she pours
an even draft of love from her core
as she crosses and recrosses the pounded floor,
unfolded and bare
to the heat, the dark, the losses.

Io

My skin is dry and creased.
For weeks the sun has drunk
the dust and blades of grasses.
This afternoon the clouds
of the morning began to cluster and
the land was overcast.

I go to the golden hill
near the cottonwood
with whipping silver leaves.
I lie beneath the cloud.
I show my breasts and close
my eyes. *Come here from the*
far green hills.

I am a cup,
a deep, empty well.
Then,
freed from every wall
in me,
a green liquor flows.

After the hardest night

from the darkened trunks
with birdsong they come
down to the pools in things
and shatter that smoothness,
scruffy from the storm water,
tossing their wings dipping,
and revel and drink and argue,
only a little, darting and
getting clean in water
that does not drown them.

I Am Your Cat

I come to your side
after hunting and curl
against your thigh
or chest to wash
myself free
of any trace
of contest and every
unnecessary seed.

Eavesdropper's Sonnet

You hear his voice inflected for her.
He flutes through consonants—
they are ashes fallen from an ember,
in Arabic; and even flattened
in pitch by some heavy news, his voice
preserves a light center, shakes
as if an incoming air current
makes him glow and remember.

Though he has reversed his pack
to hide the brand and leans in grayish
sweats, and in featureless shoes,
his voice discloses his person
entirely to the room like incense
and enters, dismantles your defenses.

Conjugal

What are these arcs of light
I sense from finger tip to
root-radicle
to fresh lattice-wings
to the nerves in bird chests
and brains to the coupling-
strong saps of spring?

Pink or golden,
they leap from point to
growth-point,
intersect in the air
of the garden and spark
where they cross, not
physically but as songs,
as the will to please another's
core and yours
in a single moment.

An hour into writing,
and the air in my palms emits
electrified stillness
like hummingbird wings.
There's a fluster in the silent
tongue, in its tip, a mix
of musics like a garden's
tastes. Its quiver lightly
loops these words we share.

The Honey Archives

In the honey,
    every circulation
        that brushed the bloom,
            the pollen, the bee,

every hint
    of flavor from each
        drop of rain
            that seeped beside
                the filamented roots,

in the honey,
   multitudes
      of blossoms, each
        laced with floral
          history, from seeds
            that formed both here
              and elsewhere,

from wars, trade
    winds, emissions,
        genetic revisions,
          the compost of given
            lives with predilections
              for certain tastes,
                from fallen native
                leaves, a repeated
                  stroke, a concentration
                  of place that you

can detect
　　in the honey,
　　　　a cast to the sweetness
　　　　　　as if it has
　　　　　　　　a transparent face
　　　　　　　　　that prints on
　　　　　　　　　　　your tongue, a key
　　　　　　　　　　　　to its identity
　　　　　　　　　　　　　　that sinks into
　　　　　　　　　　　　　　　your own, quickly,
into your bloodstream,
　　　to contour minutely
　　　　　your being to its
　　　　　　sweet locality,
　　　　　　　there is an archive
　　　　　　　　lost immediately
　　　　　　　　　into its host
　　　　　　　　　　yet never lost.

Here is
the honey archive.

It is given to
the honey of you.

In the honey
of you
the first sweetness,
the central flower
of eternal presence,
abides,
within a hum,
as if the petals
of pulsing energy
are bees
that harvest the honey
of Supreme
ecstasy.

You only need
to sink your tongue
up the back
stairway, and wait
patiently, as if
you had knelt for
days along the road
to Kailash, Mecca,
Jerusalem,
as if you had
found a love
that made the pain
of passage a refrain
of wings, another way

to taste the one
you want to find,
as if you had netted
the wind to seek
a single particle
of his hair, her left
temple, as if
your own body
were the domain
of reunion.

For every time
you taste the honey of being,
it imprints on your awareness
a memory of its vastness.

Married One

Here, I touch the two fruits in your chest.
In my translucent hand they smoke with fineness,
lilac purple, quiet-jar shapes;
they yield their scent to ardent gentleness.

As I see I want to share your name,
your skin of emerald light is close and bare.
the light is soft and sweet; the light is plain;
it means that everything is fit for care.

The Oldest Pipal Tree

After a year of hymns,
I walk through the garden in which I live
on orange gravel at sunset.

Saturate and empty,
I sing inside in a wordless way,
in the way that sorrow has
that does not expect an answer,
in which no idea holds court.
I walk, and these waves of song
go before me like open palms
feeling through rows of pipal trees
with flat, flickering leaves
till I feel her—

A silent singer can sometimes sense another's silent song.

She answers my pitched heart
and I climb to her rooted lap.
She holds my sadness in her core
and undresses it to moonlight,
commutes its roots to hers,
the oldest of loves, the nameless.
I stay with her through the blue dark,
and just before I stand,
she gives, like a mother's heirloom,
an inexhaustible seed,
set between my breasts, but deeper,
so even loss only waters
this radiant, inalienable sum.

Demolition Ophelia

—"There's rosemary, that's for remembrance. Pray you, love,
remember...
There's fennel for you, and columbines. There's rue for you,
and here's some for me..."
Ophelia, Hamlet, *Act IV, Scene V*

1

Not a precise fiction, water over ruined glory —
her white dress, her faith bequeathed to a transparent
chamber, the river pool, sealed yet flowing freely
with fish. The question of her life dissolves; her skin, her hair,
her arms are deciduous, slip like consonants
from vowels, from phrases that were sentences before,
and now murmur ah, ooo, and oh and mmm,
leaving a promise like a bouquet, a seed, a bosoming
of silence.

2

Today I see the theater with its black stage
under a scrim of clear, standing water.
The blocking of years lifts: all the players
playing roles, all their pacings, distill.
Raindrops through the roof of the house scramble
the old footsteps, mixing colors. Tomorrow
metal teeth will crumple the walls, soil
will fill the bare, smooth, concrete ear of the
audience.

3

Overcome, sometimes the day is gray
with swallowed words. She cannot direct
herself beyond her heart or speak
her will except in songs and flowers and breaking.
I feel her ash mouth now.

I have known the tenderest to break—
and cast myself alive after her back,
following her ending, and weeping for her is my oxygen.
I let her dying make an open field,
cast my certainty to compost there,
a form of god that leads through grief to wonder.

4

How did she see no way above the water?
Words must have piled up in her chest
like clutter, and broken words like stones, and rules
like hardened faces, huge hands that refuse
to budge from designs that parry and flank and scrape
power into a temporary court.
So many edifices of might decline
to serve the whole, instead see madness
in care, which forces caring into silence.
I have children, though. Flesh is
not the sacrifice that leads to truth.
The sacrifice that life requires is fear.

5

We make a circle onstage, hold a broken lyre and perform
a mirror of what was, what is, and what's to come.

6

Any who wake with ash in their mouth and fear,
imagine a clear pool and wade out with your sad objects
and let them sink, and cast in your ideas
of comfort, your cat-sized visions for a life,
your pomp about your monuments of the day,
and congratulate the worst news for undoing
borrowed, easy answers.

Sunrise, Midnight

Always sunrise on this sphere
and always midnight. We bow to both.

Saying to myself, *do not turn*
away from the death that is coming,
that is the same as to say,
do not turn away from the light.

On a day in December,
the withered tenderness of the stems,
prostrate in the frost, teaches
the bow in its harshest appearance.

And we will ask of this bow,
how do I know when to leave?
How do I know what to save?

Dream: Pilgrim Cow

I have come, the fattened pilgrim—
almost sightless, round as fruit,
loamy skin and oiled and clean,
serene as an elephantine root—

as if the slow and ornate prey
had borne itself to death and let
itself be painted gay with red
dots and ochre and draping golden cords
that her wild but placid bulk endures.

Soon the stealthy, naked women charge
from shadows to stare. They mesmerize the large
unlit bomb of lady with red triangles they flash
in arcs and they dance slow postures, sing
and hum, until the one with the fiercest breath,
with the art to aim from the contented smile,

this mustering woman blows the needle into
the mild, ample ear that does not buck;
it pierces from ear to heart and the polished person
dies, quietly incised and rolls aside,
alive for nothing else but sacrifice.

The Book I Harbor

He did laugh, but later only stared and walked throughout
that red stone land, this man whose frame was mine.

It is his book that I carry in every vestige of his skin in me—
little psychic safe houses. I am a honeycomb, tucked with
his book's mellifluous summonings, its sober lobes of ink,
its succor and raveling clarity, its treasure-feeling: the command
of that which must be salvaged.

If I lie down on a vast page will it seep out of me and resume
its wholeness? Or is my mouth its cover—its lines undone
but here recopied? Is it my womb? Is it my gait, and my way
of looking for integrity beyond bodies?

Even in Eden

A tumor's excrescence may press the esophagus,
thumb into the lungs. The throat can deform,
can close with this new lip; a creature
may die and nurse the soil with fat and bone.
You don't mind. You pervade the entire garden.

Until you distinguished that particular
apple and took to possessive separation,
death entered like any guest, shook
like any wind the creative garden. But now
you think of monuments of name, forgetting
that a lifetime's a nodule of life;
like a phantasmagoric hermit crab,

life grows through many names, houses
with vantages, you and you and you,
and when your limits wear down, you see
how life sees through every facet, enjoys
every angle, finds the freest course, and surprises.

The Valentines I Want to Write

I tuck them into the wind, but full of holes.
I have cut paper into traceries
with empty places where the words would be.
I send them; they fly, confused with clouds.
They would materialize on your palm, stranger,
and the holes would scry your heart, let
it speak to you an unerring declaration.
You would know the world adored you.
You would sense the wonder of how close
strange substances can be to a beloved.
It would unfold its tissues on your opened
palm in the wan, February light,
then blow like sugar apart, leaving your lined hand.

Serena's Hair at Two

As she nurses, I smell the hair on her head:

traces as if
of cashew butter,
pomegranate,
hickory smoke,
goat's milk,
and rubbery sweat
from our walk in the meadow

and blitzes of swallow wings,
the amplitude she lets in of sky,
fire sparks, bits of toasted marshmallow,
rubber from the vast, hot trampoline,
the dark green of this summer evening rain,
her need for umbrellas,

her hand shoved into my sleeve,
her lashes, downcast eyes,
furrowed brow as she slips her knees under
my bright pink shirt, kneading my belly with her toes, noting
the shadow shaped like a fishbone on the yellow wall,
the rustle of mice on the stove downstairs, the way she finishes
and turns away, fights off the covers, sleeps, flung
with her mouth open to the room.

Overlap

When my daughter crawls in our bed
at 2 AM and lays her bare legs
over mine, and kneads my calves with her toes
and sifts herself out that way,
I can feel the barbarous dreamscape she is leaving behind
like meal worms. Then she emits the soft,
settled state of sifted flour. Her damp
hand drags my arm over her side
and folds my elbow, tucks my hand under
her chin, and her strength transmits into my palm
her sense of rightness, and we soothe into sleep.

Cooking the News

It's noon; I cook the news.
I fuse it to battered,
sloped sunflower leaves
that endure sediments
from the sky—the moltings
of wraithlike chemical snakes,
our brown exhaust, the soot
from wildfire—and piercings
from songbird beaks.
Their broad, dirty palms
remind me: acceptance
is the ground of moral action.

I cook the rice I have—
the instants of love like collected
grain—and perfume it
with the urge to kneel and scrape
the ground, and with the last apples
overhead, still gathering
sunlight, puckering
as the tree loses more
phloem to climbing thieves.

I do not cry but work
to gather fallen fruits
and pods and withered, bleached leaves.
These I use to mulch
the strawberries. My feet
are bare on the noon-hot soil.
Their soles support my weight,
are distilling in themselves the taste
of what I have known
and what I hold as truth,
and leach that into the earth.

My equally-weighted feet
pickle the sunflower leaves
that I imagine I have plucked.
The leaves grow tender,
drawn like rags up
through my blood
through my heart to my mouth
where my tongue curls them

around the hot rice;
I can barely speak—
but eat the knowledge
of the elephant I saw
with its face hacked off,
a red scoop like
watermelon, and its
buckled knees, its back and legs
intact, kneeling,
as it lost its face.
There is brine all through
me so the leaves have gone soft.

I must eat the news,
allow that we are
not ever separate.

Harpo, the Guardian

Walking after the news, I leave the streets I know,
wander through the city, aware of the slate clouds
in the north, the moist wind through trashcans,
the breathing storm above, settling this way.
I arrive in a cul de sac, some low place, poorly planned,
beside a lot with feral grapes and a creek,
trickling between pipes, where a cooler air pulls.

He appears from behind his gate, quickly,
as if straightening from tending the climbing roses there,
then slowly, he negotiates the latch
and hails me in a rough, hushed, but free voice,
the voice of someone accustomed to largeness — of sea or horse or time.
Tethered to his oxygen tank, he exclaims
over the beauty of the day, stands with me at ease.

Are you looking for the way to the upper street, he asks.
The lost often need my help to find those hidden stairs.
I am only walking, I say. He likes this
and laughs and introduces the cats to me, then remarks
how the raccoons follow the creek, sometimes take
a cat. He motions back down the street I'd walked, saying
rogues live around that corner, too. I know them

and send them home. Keep them from that empty house;
he nods to an untended yard. *I care for the whole*
neighborhood. And I like to meet people, he admits
with a debonair smile, sweet and swift and broader
than for me. A slender girl of three dashes out a
door across the street. We stop our talk of fishing;
he listens as she chats in boisterous imperfection,

swinging on, then clinging to the chain link fence,
pale cheeks pressed to the metal, unsure but keen
eyes. We exchange the simplest phrases, then, quiet,
she lolls then drags herself around. He points to his reaching

peas, so lithely delicate, jubilantly abandoned
in this August heat, and beyond to his lemon cucumbers.
Harpo draws a few steps from his legs

like a long, slow revelation from under a silk scarf.
He wants to give me some, says they turn, get a radiant
blush of yellow-green at the stem, and you have to pick them
then or the seeds mature and there is no more fruit.
That's good for the plant, he adds, but these are good for you.
Then he pauses, calls to the girl, *That is too high*
and she slides her feet back to earth.

Autumn 2017

The new wind makes a tossing sea as
debris bucks off the rattle-dry limbs of the acacias
and filaments roll in the air like seaweed in surf past the
kitchen window where I scrub pans. When I

go outside, I stand barefoot on the hot,
irregular concrete of the 1930s. I face
the bleaching sun of noon, and that wind carries
the tinder-box spice of the valley—that bulge of pumpkins
out from under fans of yellowed leaves, that fatness
on one side, thinness on the other. In this wind

from the shambles of this year, I accept my thickened belly
more, its fold of fat, and the weathering of the skin
on my hands; my features match the creases and swelling
and dishevelment of autumn, I cannot reject the laboring
of plants, now yellow and bitten and going brittle,
the shredded, withering grapes, pecked by birds, these
sagging things that coincide with fullness.

Dream: Resolve

Dulled by sweets and fat, you dream
of Nordic women, ashen, with green-tinged
shadows, who swim the churning surf
between blue ice and rock.

One, with a ponderous belly but
gloriously happy eyes, wades
out to tell her lover *good morning,*
then wades back,
naked into the arctic channel.

That is a woman, a real woman,
he thinks, her lover on the shore.
A terrifying woman, her white
hair with a little gold, swept
into a carefree knot,

she disappears into the water
like a whale
unburdened by its power, dives
into the heavy and darkening sea
without collapse or loss of song.

Columns

With mercy like a bolt through the blue morning,
the nurse in white gathers his charge and order.
The uniform avows he is a bud
swollen on a spring branch whose palm
will open and absorb in its living rag
a little of the stuff we cannot breathe and
give the oxygen feed, the hand we need
to brush when we are so alone in the hush
of the hospital, and we do not know what
to do with all the love that still remains.

How can we think our happiness depends
on comfy sofas, things that whir and obey?

He obeys the way a column does.
Its stone was shaped by hundreds who were shaped by centuries
of others who came to know the space to leave
between each ridge, and how to taper the stone
so it springs, unavoidably abstract, an essence
of grace on you, grace calculated
from unfurling leaves and seed heads.
He obeys the clear sight that calculates
the right support, this moment, your opening hand.

Murmurate

Our thoughts murmurate around the globe.
Like thoughts sweep with like. The kindred
wheel, drift and converge as they map
through billions of minds our consonant themes.
So we, a massive will, brush the Earth
as starlings flex through the sky in one stroke.

Yet, if we veer toward a lie, a cage,
toward the will to refuse scarred hands,
if we curve our sight in fear, acting
the day hawk ready to dive,
who can overrule our bleakest patterns
as they compound into covenants of habit?

Land. Quieted on a branch, perceive
the last of this coursing thought from your
wounded self, ruddy with fighting for the golden
apple, fallen blind to union, bound
to name, pain accumulating in your eyes
that tips, sometimes, riots into a hawkish dark
arrow bearing down on the village.

This insight folds a thought back into itself,
makes the sight the thought and so undoes
its aim, and absorbs its force in unchanging fullness.
Knowing women have spoken this, men have written it,
whales have sung what you hold in your heart, wholly
open, our movements become movements of peace.

What the Road Has to Say

One in black tatters
bends as if into wind
with arms locked forward
to drive the shabby pram
through this windless morning
over the asphalt overpass,
slowly, starving slow.

The displaced speak to me,
They curl on me.
I have no food but litter.
I cannot soften,
cannot reply except
through ramps and curbs,
and roadkill carcasses.

See the mother duck,
neck aloft, shocked,
white-eyed on the berm,
webbed feet on noon asphalt,
her ducklings placidly jostling
around her, and the drake
swivels to catch her glance.

If I could plait ramps of grass
over me to let them pass,
overpasses with fruiting shrubs,
fenceless overpasses
with shelters for our homeless,
I would. But people do not see
as clearly as I do.

Barn Swallows

Those two have
pressed together
a heavier vellum
of earth and grass
into a cupping nest
and flight's the invisible
letter
that tells, with a gorgeous
emptiness,
of full mouths.

Their arcs,
like bows tied
with returns,
have my husband
pulled up in wonder
like one of the young
to watch the young
wide beaks
he has only seen
in cartoons.

Four Cats

We hear the cat wondering
loudly to the gate
he *could* slip through,
if he would follow us
past what is safe.

We walk along the road,
summer heat around the ankles
even at sunset.
The sky has thickened with wildfire smut,
is golden and, we feel, weary.
We talk

again about the weight of stories,
our stories,
walking past the yards of
everyone's reflections of hope
or value: trees trimmed to simple geometry
or swollen to languorous fruit,
a pot with a puppy face, live dogs,
and a cat, so fluffy
yet petite the earth must hardly feel her.

She steps as if along a tightrope,
tail raised in salutation.
Our daughter would want her,
has wanted her, drawn her,
has wished away our cat for her.

We continue up the steepest part,
and I have said that I no longer have a story
and without this sense of arc
the days are better, small matchings,
like the meal I carried across the field

to the homeless man in the limp, tan car,
who said that he had just prayed for maybe
a bit more food that night after his can of beans,
who seemed spooked to see the plate appear.

These matchings are enough.
You like this idea, weary of wanting setbacks
to lead to greater purpose.
But you tease me for exclaiming
at the roses ahead, decorously disheveled.
We do stop together to greet another

cat, this one lean, short-haired, and exactly
the color of the graying asphalt.
It steps its way from under a car to us,
to flop on its side, its finely arched brows
above closed eyes, letting us rub its neck.
It is so much more approachable
than our own, we say.

Then it rises, slips to the roadside,
and we are excused.
We turn left, the turn toward home.
As we walk, feeling our hips, our feet,
you say your essential doubt,
which I cannot remember now,
but then, as I paused, gathering a response
from all my years, leaving
aside the wishes,
before I could speak, another cat,

a fluffy black one, detaches
from the unkempt grass beside the street,
and calls to us.
You doubt that it wants to meet you
turn away,
but this is the one who wants you only.
Passing me with the briefest nuzzle,
it goes to your feet and drops its head sideways
against your toes and licks them.
So you giggle; it lifts and circles
and drops onto your other foot and licks it.
Even as you titter and almost jump
the cat is content to rub and circle,
until it leaves you and barely grazes my leg
on the way back to the grass.

From the Snowstorm on Clay Street

Last winter I stood in a snowstorm—the cold, fast-coming cloak over color, the silent settling of so much out of control.

I entered, hunched for warmth. But when I raised my face to the flakes, they struck more like kisses, hard then softening into a ragged lace of slush on my skin. I felt instead the delicate fists of them, felt those knotted forms as features to be known. They were falling, and I was below them. We were meeting. They were doing only what they do, spinning constellated, adrift, like skirts without dancers, a whole air of them from a strangely sepia cloud, obeying temperatures.

Today, I got the call. The temperature dropped. A flurry of things formed, just so, which I cannot change. But I choose not to slip through my life hunched over as if I can ever avoid these sorts of blows, kisses.

The Day Mandela Died

Now, these years, with tinsel through my hair, my grandmother
sits, hands slackened between her thighs, and watches

the wash of sunlight through my mother's window; *that
is beautiful*, she says, in her empty wasp-nest voice,
all day the wind has shaken the shadows on the walls
and the potted flowers glow, *it has been so quick, this day,*
she says, at last, *I am so happy just to sit and watch.*

But in my sorrow I washed two towels with the delicates
and in my rush to fix the sheets, I left the door ajar
and the heat goes out that my husband wanted in, and that is like before,
when the cat ran wild from the opened cage into the winter wood,
with his limp, at dusk, he cried in answer, but no longer came to my hands.

What hands can do, that is what has passed from her
and both sun and shadow flash with glory like accomplishments;
but she does not wrestle with her powers anymore
and can enjoy the whole in passive gratitude.
I wonder how my death will be; that I may sit in sunlight,

warm with impartial heat, bony frame wrapped in a shawl
and the last glimpse is of red, lit leaves.
This is a way I might let light usher me out,
as if the sun's pressure became more real
than the stories in these busy bones.

Tonight, I wrap beside my sleepy daughter,
hold her moist, plump hand, again,
sing, dee, dee, dee, and swing low
sweet chariot, coming for to carry, and
she asks for me to stay a little longer.

I Was There to See

The rain spackled the road with mirrors,
whipped yellow flags from dark limbs,
plastered the ground with solemn, happy paper, the frogs sang

until the silent, golden sun
through massive drifts displayed forms
with wind in their sliding architecture, and marked with light

their subtlest frays, intricate,
mutable, their chasms and shadows.
I stood as the salmon light stayed, as the storm loosened

and blue was with the rose above a fan of gold
and the heavy old apple trees, the laborious
twists in the darkening oaks, the lit new grass, all

glittered in the rosy end. How grateful,
how little it mattered the idea
of deserving: I was there to see.

Fabric

There, the shimmery, the matte cotton, the frayed, the tufted,
the mass of fabric scraps that she won't throw away, is my mother
who fingers fabrics sideways, not turning till she wants a length;
she keeps her scraps, the color field, the pool of individuals
apart, tousled to rouse her sense of depth, the potency
the field reflects: this with this with this and that or that.

Last night I dreamed a pile of fabric scraps, a fabulous pink
metallic wing, a ginger wool, greens of undersides,
and flashes of tips of more, a mound a woman formed, to save
and give away to me the chance to bring the scraps together;
and here I see my lists as colors: the Sanskrit lover, gardener,
mother, poet, the stomps I dance, the tendency to sit
and watch a while, translator without fluency...

or see the field of gorgeous skins: the russet, the burnt umber,
the pale of pith, the faintest yellow as the cast of a set sun,
the shiny loamy ones, the bone, the unglazed porcelain,
the scaly green, the silver wet, the white fur, the roan...
as if pieced together to form a quilt whose seams reveal
binding life, a whole that shifts together, flows and rests.

The Bow

Here the student bows, whitening daily
in the gray space, the unfurnished chamber;
a day's breezes hardly ruffle her hair
but pendular changes like sea waves sweep.

The student bows and spills a head
of patterns—dashes or dots or stitching
onto the floor, in waves of undoing.
Her yellows, blacks, blues, and reds,

the colors the student claimed, flow
forth. She feels the waves swing on the white
hinge, feels the hinge all the time,
all things touching that, everywhere she goes.

It's Not Mine

The broad shine on this pitted street comforts me—
a dimpled gold that no one can hoard.

And the newspaper, layers sloughed into the weeds, comforts me—
like marks on birch bark: the typeset and the peach of ads gone to mush.

And the smoke from chimneys, in guffaws,
hovers and loosens, spins widely to where no one stands to watch.

And the sheen of a manzanita that is not mine to prune,
and the pile of requirements, too,

the list, that comes to me like a weather of necessity,
comforts me since I have no story to believe, here at the beginning.

Jerusalem Now

And see her wild hair is the wind; the day of crossed scents
  on the hill adorns her
as here blows feral rosemary, daphne and rose, and bitter
  hawthorn and musty
broken leaves, and tar fumes and snot and semen and musk
  glands of snakes and
the sweat of the city and the depleted country, the bitters of
  smoke. She,
Jerusalem, will greet her lover, anywhere.

Smell her hands within the fire, in the bakery, in the gym, the
  court, the temple.
She is the field of scent devoid of preference. See her newly-◄
  woven gown like the
table, the bed, the screen. See her heaving every sinusoid.
  She is the field of vision
devoid of preference. Touch her wherever your blood flows and
  however your skin
pricks. Hear her bridal shudder, louder, louder, into words and
  meandering sounds.
She feeds herself to you, anything at your lips can be known
  as Jerusalem. You
choose to savor her in a limited way as your own flesh or as
  every body.

This Jerusalem of every city, her flesh of every sidewalk,
  is unveiled to the
gentlest footfalls, to those who know she's there. And they
  shake and shudder
freely anywhere. And wail or kneel or sing or do what they
  must do, but with an
undeterred smile, these lovers.

And does she stand, shimmering at the southern border? White
  gown in the red dirt
that we tread on the bridge, she, the damsel who some fight
  the dragon-

immigrants as if to save, stands among the immigrants, unseen
  by the newest patrol.
A shimmer like heat, she waits with us. She, the mothers and
  fathers who shade
their children with their bodies, whose sweat anoints them. She
  is the shiver
through the mind that checks fear, that opens the way for care
  at 9 AM, at 9:15
then 10, at noon at midnight at 9 AM again.

And the patrolling soldiers hear her cries—the children in cages
  cry mama,
mama! In their skin, the agents feel the urge to stoop, to sacrifice
  their badges and
stoop and gather them into their arms and find, through mazes of
  paper and
questions and walking and apologies, their mothers, their fathers,
  the child's
Jerusalem. But they lie to cover the urges. They call the children
  instruments
played, an orchestra, then a bunch of horns to silence. But that is
  Jerusalem,
the beloved place, mislaid, misconceived, abandoned at the altar.
  A different knot tied.

And is she revealed in the loose gowns of jellyfish that hover
  where the ocean
dies? Is she regal in the clutter of satellites and trash within
  the planetary orbit?
Does she stride forward across the cleared Amazon with cow
  hooves round her
neck? Or with the slowed atmospheric river like a draping boa?
  None of these
are her wedding gown. These mark how we refuse her, but still
  she exists,
jangling the trash and trashed like a mirror-gown that catches
  our eye like
nagging, or as an echo catches the ear and makes you attentive.
  You want to find
her, even there. You want to shed the blindness of suffering and
  set aside

demands and see her. You want to go to Jerusalem. You want
  a place to kneel.
A pure place. Her bridal descent. A place without any contaminant,
  not even a
trace of pollution. Not a jot of separation. The site of reunion.

And now if the bride emerges, Jerusalem, in every city, on every
  lane, and the
dingy wastes we amassed erupt as art as she emerges, like butterflies
  the dark,
sullen heaps will develop into apologies: kodachrome valances of
  plastic, pillars of
marbled plastic from melted straws, prosthetic arms from
  salvaged waste,
microbes we cultivate will eat the traces and the cleaned ocean
  will sway and
bask and grow new swaths of plankton.

Author Biography

Alicia Vandevorst has written poetry for thirty years and formally studied with Patricia Donegan, Maxine Kumin, Barbara Jordan, and with Arthur Sze at the Napa Valley Writers' Conference in 2012. Her poems have appeared in *The American Poetry Journal, Canary: A Literary Journal of the Environmental Crisis, Writing in a Woman's Voice, and Sisyphus.* She also writes more experimental performance pieces. While attending Scripps College, she wrote and produced a poem for four voices, *In'erstates,* and provided dance-chants for *Nucleus Expansion,* a collaboration between the Dance and Ceramics Departments. More recently, she completed a play titled Psyche that combines poetry and theater, meditation and mask-work and served as a playwright for the 24 Hour Plays in Nevada City. Her poetry and writing have three companion practices: meditation, photography, and composting.

www.ingramcontent.com/pod-product-compliance
Lightning Source LLC
Chambersburg PA
CBHW081134090426
42737CB00018B/3340